Finding Your Voice

Overcoming Verbal Abuse

21-Day Journal

M L Ruscsak

Trient Press
3375 S Rainbow Blvd
#81710, SMB 13135
Las Vegas,NV 89180

Ordering Information:
Quantity sales. Special discounts are available on quantity purchases by corporations, associations, and others. For details, contact the publisher at the address above.
Orders by U.S. trade bookstores and wholesalers. Please contact Trient Press: Tel: (775) 996-3844; or visit www.trientpress.com.

Printed in the United States of America

Publisher's Cataloging-in-Publication data
Ruscsak, M.L.
A title of a book : Finding Your Voice: Overcoming Verbal Abuse 21-day journal
ISBN
Paperback   978-1-955198-85-1
E-book   978-1-955198-91-2

Journal Exercise:

Write down your reasons for starting this journaling journey.

_____
_____
_____
_____
_____
_____
_____
_____
_____
_____
_____
_____
_____
_____
_____

What motivated you to pick up this book and begin this journey of self-discovery and healing?

_____
_____
_____
_____
_____
_____
_____
_____
_____
_____
_____
_____
_____
_____
_____
_____

Reflect on your expectations and what you hope to gain from this experience. Think about what you hope to learn, what you hope to achieve, and what you hope to feel after completing the 21 days. Write down your thoughts and feelings, and be honest with yourself.

Remember, this is a journey, and it's okay to have high hopes, but also be realistic about what you hope to accomplish. This journal is a safe space for you to reflect, process, and grow, and it will be here to support you every step of the way.

any experiences you may have had with verbal abuse. This can be in your personal or professional life, or both. Write down your thoughts and feelings about these experiences, and what impact they had on you.

_____
_____
_____
_____
_____
_____
_____
_____
_____
_____
_____
_____
_____
_____
_____
_____
_____
_____
_____
_____
_____
_____
_____
_____

Write down what you already know about verbal abuse and what you want to learn: Make a list of what you already know about verbal abuse and what you hope to learn from this journaling journey. Consider any questions or concerns you have, and what you hope to gain from your exploration.

_____
_____
_____
_____
_____
_____

By reflecting on your experiences and understanding of verbal abuse, you will be better equipped to navigate the challenges and opportunities of your healing journey.

Take some time to think about the different ways that verbal abuse can manifest. This can include things like name-calling, belittling comments, constant criticism, or threatening language. Consider how these types of abuse can impact someone emotionally, mentally, and physically.

Write down examples of verbal abuse you have experienced or witnessed:
Think about your own experiences with verbal abuse.

_____
_____
_____
_____
_____
_____
_____
_____
_____
_____
_____
_____
_____
_____
_____
_____
_____
_____
_____
_____
_____
_____
_____
_____
_____
_____
_____
_____
_____

_____
_____
_____
_____
_____
_____
_____
_____
_____
_____
_____
_____
_____
_____
_____
_____
_____
_____
_____
_____
_____
_____
_____
_____
_____
_____
_____
_____
_____
_____
_____

Consider the effects that these incidents had on you and how they still impact you today. This exercise is an opportunity to begin to understand the ways that verbal abuse has affected you and your life.

Reflect and Write: Take a moment to reflect on how verbal abuse has affected you. Write down the ways that verbal abuse has impacted your thoughts, emotions, and actions. Consider how it has shaped your self-esteem, and what aspects of your life have been most affected.

_____
_____
_____
_____
_____
_____
_____
_____
_____
_____
_____
_____
_____
_____
_____
_____
_____
_____
_____
_____
_____
_____
_____
_____
_____
_____
_____
_____
_____
_____
_____

_____

_____

_____

_____

_____

_____

_____

_____

_____

_____

_____

_____

_____

_____

_____

_____

_____

_____

_____

_____

_____

_____

_____

_____

_____

_____

_____

_____

_____

_____

Looking Forward: Use this opportunity to look forward and set a goal for what you hope to achieve through your journey of healing and self-discovery. Write down what you want to work towards in terms of building a healthier and more fulfilling life for yourself.

Take some time to read about the cycle of abuse and how it relates to your experiences with verbal abuse. Think about the patterns you have noticed in your own experiences with verbal abuse.

_____
_____
_____
_____
_____
_____
_____
_____
_____
_____
_____
_____
_____
_____
_____
_____
_____

Breaking the Cycle:
Write down your thoughts and feelings about breaking the cycle of abuse. What steps can you take to break this cycle and reclaim your power?

_____
_____
_____
_____
_____
_____
_____
_____
_____
_____
_____
_____
_____
_____
_____
_____

_____
_____
_____
_____
_____
_____
_____
_____
_____
_____
_____
_____
_____
_____

Moving Forward:
Write a letter to yourself, addressing the person you were when you were in the cycle of abuse.

_____
_____
_____
_____
_____
_____
_____
_____
_____
_____
_____
_____
_____
_____
_____

Encourage yourself to take the steps necessary to break the cycle and move forward. Reflect on your strengths and the progress you have already made in your healing journey.

By reflecting on the cycle of abuse and taking steps to break it, you are taking control of your life and moving towards a future where you are safe and in control.

will be a source of encouragement and understanding.

Exercise:
List of Support:

Write down a list of friends, family members, or professionals you can reach out to for help during this process.

_____
_____
_____
_____
_____
_____
_____
_____
_____
_____
_____
_____
_____
_____
_____

Think about the qualities you value in a supportive person, such as empathy, active listening, and understanding.

_____
_____
_____
_____
_____
_____
_____
_____
_____
_____
_____
_____
_____

_____
_____
_____
_____
_____
_____
_____
_____
_____
_____
_____
_____
_____
_____
_____
_____
_____
_____

Write down the ways you can reach out to each person for support, such as through phone calls, text messages, or in-person conversations.

_____
_____
_____
_____
_____
_____
_____
_____
_____
_____
_____
_____
_____
_____
_____

Remember, having a strong support system can make a big difference in your healing process, so don't be afraid to reach out to others for help.

life and the impact it has had on your thoughts, emotions, and actions.

Writing Exercise:

Write down strategies for coping with the aftermath of verbal abuse and reducing its impact on your life.

_____
_____
_____
_____
_____
_____
_____
_____
_____
_____
_____
_____
_____
_____

Think about what has helped you in the past when dealing with difficult emotions and what you can incorporate into your daily routine to help manage the effects of trauma.

_____
_____
_____
_____
_____
_____
_____
_____
_____
_____
_____
_____
_____

What self-care practices can you engage in to help you cope with the aftermath of abuse?

_____
_____
_____
_____
_____
_____
_____
_____
_____
_____
_____
_____
_____
_____
_____
_____

What activities bring you comfort and help you manage stress?

_____
_____
_____
_____
_____
_____
_____
_____
_____
_____
_____
_____
_____
_____
_____

What are some healthy ways to manage your emotions when you feel overwhelmed?

_____
_____

_____
_____
_____
_____
_____
_____
_____
_____
_____
_____

How can you create a safe and supportive environment for yourself during this healing journey?

_____
_____
_____
_____
_____
_____
_____
_____
_____
_____
_____
_____
_____
_____
_____
_____

Take some time to review your list and prioritize the strategies that resonate with you the most. Consider reaching out to someone you trust for additional support and guidance as you work to cope with the aftermath of verbal abuse and reduce its impact on your life.

Spend some time thinking about the idea of reclaiming your power and what that means to you.

Consider the impact of verbal abuse on your life and how it has affected your sense of control and agency.

Reflect on why it is important for you to reclaim your power and what that could look like for you.

Writing:

Write down your thoughts and reflections on the idea of reclaiming your power.

_____
_____
_____
_____
_____
_____
_____
_____
_____
_____
_____
_____
_____
_____
_____
_____
_____
_____

Make a list of what reclaiming your power could mean for you in practical terms.

_____
_____
_____
_____
_____
_____
_____
_____
_____
_____
_____

for yourself, or making choices that align with your values.

_____
_____
_____
_____
_____
_____
_____
_____
_____
_____
_____
_____
_____
_____
_____
_____
_____
_____
_____
_____
_____
_____

Consider the steps you can take to start reclaiming your power. This could be something as simple as saying "no" to something that doesn't align with your values or reaching out for help when you need it.

_____
_____
_____
_____
_____
_____
_____
_____
_____
_____
_____
_____
_____

_____

_____

_____

_____

_____

_____

_____

_____

Write a personal statement or affirmations to remind yourself of the importance of reclaiming your power and your commitment to doing so.

_____

_____

_____

_____

_____

_____

_____

_____

_____

_____

_____

_____

_____

_____

_____

_____

_____

_____

_____

_____

and express yourself.
Think about how important it is for you to reclaim your voice and start speaking up for yourself.
Writing Exercise:

Write down your thoughts and feelings about finding your voice. How does this concept make you feel?

_____
_____
_____
_____
_____
_____
_____
_____
_____
_____
_____
_____
_____
_____
_____
_____
_____

Think about the steps you can take to build confidence in your voice and assert yourself. Write down specific actions you can take to start speaking up and expressing yourself more confidently.

_____
_____
_____
_____
_____
_____
_____
_____
_____
_____
_____
_____

confidence. Write down the people, resources, or activities that you can turn to for support and encouragement.

_____

_____

_____

_____

_____

_____

_____

_____

_____

_____

_____

_____

_____

_____

_____

_____

_____

_____

_____

_____

_____

_____

_____

Consider your fears and obstacles that may prevent you from speaking up. Write down ways you can overcome these fears and challenges.

_____

_____

_____

_____

_____

_____

_____

_____

_____

_____

_____

_____

_____

_____

_____

_____

Think about your future self, where you have found your voice and are able to speak up and assert yourself confidently. Write down what this future version of yourself looks like and what you hope to achieve.

_____

_____

_____

_____

_____

_____

_____

_____

_____

_____

_____

_____

_____

_____

_____

_____

_____

_____

_____

_____

_____

about this fear and how it affects your ability to assert yourself and reclaim your power.

_____
_____
_____
_____
_____
_____
_____
_____
_____
_____
_____
_____
_____
_____
_____
_____
_____

Write down ways to overcome this fear:
Think about what you can do to overcome this fear and build confidence in your voice. This could include practicing self-care and self-compassion, seeking support from friends, family, or a therapist, or learning assertiveness skills.

_____
_____
_____
_____
_____
_____
_____
_____
_____
_____
_____
_____
_____
_____
_____
_____

Write down any ideas that come to mind and which ones you would like to explore further.

Remember, reclaiming your power and finding your voice is a journey and it is okay to take baby steps. Every effort you make, no matter how small, is an important step in the right direction.

_____
_____
_____
_____
_____
_____
_____
_____
_____
_____
_____
_____
_____
_____
_____
_____
_____
_____

Write down your thoughts and feelings about self-care.

_____
_____
_____
_____
_____
_____
_____
_____
_____
_____
_____
_____
_____
_____
_____
_____

Understanding the Importance of Self-Care: Verbal abuse can take a toll on our mental and emotional well-being. It is important to take care of ourselves in order to heal and move forward. Write down why self-care is important for your personal growth and healing.

_____
_____

_____
_____
_____
_____
_____
_____
_____
_____
_____
_____
_____

Incorporating Self-Care into Your Daily Routine: Think about three activities or self-care practices you can incorporate into your daily routine. This could be anything from reading a book, going for a walk, practicing yoga, or taking a relaxing bath. Write down these three self-care practices and make a commitment to yourself to do them regularly.

_____
_____
_____
_____
_____
_____
_____
_____
_____
_____
_____
_____
_____
_____
_____
_____

Remember, self-care is a crucial aspect of healing from verbal abuse. By taking care of yourself, you are showing yourself love, compassion, and respect. You are also giving yourself the time and space you need to heal and grow.

healing and growth. I am proud of you for making this commitment to yourself and for taking this important step towards reclaiming your power and finding your voice.

I hope that this journal has provided you with the tools and support you need to understand the impact of verbal abuse and start moving forward. You have already accomplished so much, and I have no doubt that you will continue to make progress as you continue on this journey.

Remember to be kind to yourself and celebrate each small victory along the way. You are doing an amazing job, and I am honored to be a part of your journey towards healing, growth, and self-discovery.

Sincerely,

M. L. Ruscsak

_____
_____
_____
_____
_____
_____
_____
_____
_____
_____
_____
_____
_____
_____
_____

What do you believe are your strengths and weaknesses?

_____
_____
_____
_____
_____
_____
_____
_____
_____
_____
_____
_____
_____
_____

Take some time to reflect on your confidence levels and where you would like to see growth.

Journal Exercise:

Goals for building confidence: Write down your goals for building confidence.

_____
_____
_____
_____
_____
_____
_____
_____
_____
_____
_____
_____

What do you hope to achieve and how will increased confidence benefit you?

_____
_____
_____
_____
_____
_____
_____
_____
_____
_____
_____
_____
_____
_____
_____
_____

Steps to achieve your goals: Write down the steps you can take to reach your confidence-building goals. This may include practicing self-affirmations, trying new activities, or seeking support from others.

_____
_____
_____
_____
_____
_____
_____
_____

_____
_____
_____
_____
_____
_____
_____
_____

Action plan: Create an action plan for how you will work towards your confidence-building goals. This could include setting achievable milestones, planning regular check-ins with yourself, or seeking feedback from others.

_____
_____
_____
_____
_____
_____
_____
_____
_____
_____
_____
_____
_____
_____
_____
_____
_____
_____
_____
_____

Remember, building confidence takes time and effort, but it's a journey worth pursuing. Be kind to yourself and celebrate your progress along the way!

how it can help you heal. What are your thoughts and feelings about this process? Are you feeling resistant or open to accepting your past experiences? Write down your thoughts and feelings about this process.

Exercise:

Write down steps you can take to start accepting your past experiences and moving forward. Here are a few suggestions to get you started:

Practice self-compassion and talk to yourself with kindness and understanding.
Acknowledge and validate your experiences, emotions, and feelings.
Surround yourself with supportive friends, family members, or professionals who understand your experiences and offer encouragement and support.
Write letters to those who have hurt you and process your emotions through writing.
Engage in therapy or other forms of support to help you heal from the aftermath of verbal abuse.

_____
_____
_____
_____
_____
_____
_____
_____
_____
_____
_____
_____
_____
_____
_____
_____
_____

Remember, accepting your past experiences is a process and it's okay to take it one step at a time. Celebrate your progress and be proud of yourself for taking this important step towards healing.

healing. It's important to recognize the importance of letting go of the pain and hurt from verbal abuse.

Write:

Reflect on the pain and hurt you have experienced as a result of verbal abuse. Write down why it's important to let go of this pain and hurt.

_____
_____
_____
_____
_____
_____
_____
_____
_____
_____
_____
_____
_____
_____
_____
_____
_____
_____
_____
_____
_____
_____
_____
_____

List down the ways you can start letting go of the pain and hurt. Consider methods such as forgiveness, mindfulness, and therapy.

_____
_____
_____
_____
_____

Write a letter to yourself or the person who has caused you pain, expressing your feelings and forgiving them, or simply acknowledging the pain and letting it go.

your life and mental well-being.

_____
_____
_____
_____
_____
_____
_____
_____
_____
_____
_____
_____
_____
_____
_____
_____
_____
_____
_____
_____
_____
_____
_____

associated with verbal abuse, but with the right support and guidance, it is possible to heal and move forward.

Write down your thoughts:

Why do you think therapy and support are important for your healing process?

_____
_____
_____
_____
_____
_____
_____
_____
_____
_____
_____
_____
_____
_____
_____
_____
_____
_____
_____
_____
_____
_____
_____

Have you considered seeking therapy or support for the effects of verbal abuse in your life? If so, why? If not, why not?

_____
_____
_____
_____
_____

What do you hope to gain from therapy or support? Do you have any specific goals in mind?

_____
_____
_____
_____
_____
_____
_____
_____
_____
_____
_____
_____
_____
_____
_____
_____
_____
_____
_____
_____
_____
_____
_____
_____
_____
_____
_____
_____

Take the time to reflect on your experiences and thoughts on therapy and support, and write down your insights. Remember, taking this step towards seeking help is a powerful and brave action towards healing and reclaiming your power.

in the past, what you would like to try, and what you still need to work on.

Writing Exercise:

Write down a list of the strategies for coping that you have tried or are aware of. Reflect on what has worked for you and what has not.

_____
_____
_____
_____
_____
_____
_____
_____
_____
_____
_____
_____
_____
_____
_____
_____
_____
_____
_____
_____
_____
_____

Think about what you would like to try in the future or what you still need to work on.

_____
_____
_____
_____
_____
_____

Write down a plan for incorporating new coping strategies into your life and making progress in your healing journey.

Write down ways you can start showing love and compassion to yourself and practicing self-care on a daily basis.

What steps can you take to start loving and accepting yourself fully, despite your past experiences with verbal abuse?

_____

_____

_____

_____

_____

_____

_____

_____

_____

_____

_____

_____

_____

_____

_____

_____

_____

_____

_____

_____

Verbal abuse can leave us feeling disempowered and lacking control in our lives. However, reclaiming our power is an essential step towards healing and regaining our sense of self.

Reflection:

Think about your past experiences with verbal abuse and how they have shaped your understanding of power and control.
Consider what reclaiming your power could mean for you and your life.

_____
_____
_____
_____
_____
_____
_____
_____
_____
_____
_____
_____
_____
_____
_____
_____
_____
_____
_____
_____

Writing:

Write down a list of actions you can take to start reclaiming your power and finding your voice. Some examples may include:
a. Setting healthy boundaries in your relationships

_____

_____
_____
_____
_____
_____
_____
_____
_____
_____
_____
_____
_____
_____
_____
_____
_____
_____
_____

b. Practicing assertiveness and speaking up for yourself

_____
_____
_____
_____
_____
_____
_____
_____
_____
_____
_____
_____
_____
_____
_____
_____
_____
_____
_____
_____

c. Pursuing hobbies or activities that bring you joy and help you feel empowered

_____

_____

_____

_____

_____

_____

_____

_____

_____

_____

_____

_____

_____

_____

_____

_____

_____

_____

_____

_____

_____

d. Challenging negative self-talk and beliefs that hold you back

_____

_____

_____

_____

_____

_____

_____

_____

_____

e. Surrounding yourself with supportive and empowering people

Remember, reclaiming your power is a journey, and it takes time and effort. But it is a crucial step towards healing and finding inner peace and happiness.

_____

_____

_____

_____

_____

_____

_____

_____

_____

_____

_____

_____

_____

_____

_____

_____

_____

_____

_____

_____

Identify any limiting beliefs or self-doubt that may be holding you back from speaking up

_____

_____

_____

_____

_____

_____

_____

_____

_____

_____

_____

_____

_____
_____
_____
_____
_____
_____
_____
_____
_____
_____

Practice assertiveness and setting boundaries by role-playing a difficult conversation or scenario

Write down your thoughts and feelings about finding your voice and speaking up against verbal abuse, including any fears or obstacles you may be facing. Reflect on how you can continue to build your confidence and assertiveness in the face of challenges.

_____
_____
_____
_____
_____
_____
_____
_____
_____
_____
_____
_____
_____
_____
_____
_____
_____
_____

Consider what steps you can take to practice speaking up in safe, low-stakes situations, and how you can prepare yourself for more difficult conversations in the future.

_____

_____

_____

_____

_____

_____

_____

_____

_____

_____

_____

_____

_____

_____

_____

_____

_____

_____

_____

_____

_____

_____

_____

Challenge any negative self-talk or beliefs that are preventing you from speaking up and asserting yourself. Write down these beliefs and reframe them in a positive light. For example, if you believe that speaking up will only result in retaliation, remind yourself of past experiences where you have spoken up and the outcome was positive.

_____

_____

_____

_____

_____

_____

_____

_____

_____
_____
_____
_____
_____
_____
_____
_____
_____
_____
_____
_____
_____
_____
_____

Write a letter to your future self, affirming your strengths and your ability to assert yourself in any situation. Remind yourself of the progress you have made and how far you have come. Celebrate your growth and the steps you have taken to build self-confidence and overcome the fear of retaliation. Encourage yourself to continue on this journey and to never give up on your goals.

_____
_____
_____
_____
_____
_____
_____
_____
_____
_____
_____
_____
_____
_____
_____
_____
_____
_____
_____
_____

Prepare yourself by visualizing the situation and the outcome you want

_____
_____
_____
_____
_____
_____
_____
_____

Take the opportunity to practice speaking up and expressing your thoughts and feelings, using the skills you have learned throughout the journal.

_____
_____
_____
_____
_____
_____
_____
_____
_____
_____
_____
_____
_____
_____
_____
_____
_____
_____
_____
_____
_____
_____
_____
_____

Write down your thoughts and feelings about the situation before and after you speak up, and how it felt to assert yourself. Reflect on what you learned from this experience and how you can continue to use these skills in the future.

_____